A Journey of Love with BABY PANDA

REBECCA T. URRUTIA

____

This book belongs to.

____

If lost, please return to Name ___________________________

Address: ____

City and State ____________________________________

Contact information _______________________________

Parents contact information at work _______________

Parents email address: ____________________________

Parents phone numbers _____________________________

Family Doctor phone _______________________________

A JOURNEY OF LOVE WITH BABY PANDA

The baby panda woke up to a fantastic sunrise. He climbed out of the cave to enjoy the day. He watched a butterfly fluttering around, and it landed on his paw. It was glimmering and flashing on and off, and then it flew away.

With a spring in his step, the playful baby panda followed the butterfly for hours along different paths, and he was not paying attention, then the forest grew darker. He now found himself at the ocean shore, where the ocean breezes whipped around his face, and he whimpered, "Where am I?"

He looked around. No one was there. He wept because he did not know where he was.

His sobbing grew louder and louder. Then a baby harp seal approached him and asked," Why are you crying?"

Baby Panda said, "I am lost now, I will never see my mother again,"

The baby harp seal asked, "Well, which direction did you come from?"

Baby Panda said, "I don't know. I followed a beautiful butterfly."

"I have never seen anything like you; what are you?" asked the baby harp seal.

"I am a baby panda bear," the baby panda answered.

"I have never seen anything like you either."

"What are you, and where do you live?"

I am a baby harp seal. I live around rocky shorelines where we are now."

"It's nice to meet you," replied baby panda bear.

A penguin passed by and asked, "What's going on here?"

Baby panda is lost. We should help him," answered baby harp seal.

"Baby panda, this is a penguin, and she lives here too, "said baby harp seal.

Baby panda did not say hello. He continued to cry, and his wailing attracted several more animals.

Flying fishes jumped in and out of the water, yelling, "What is going on?"

"We are going to help baby panda. He lost his mother," baby harp seal explained.

Then, a pelican flew in and landed on the sand next to a baby panda.

All the animals chattered, "How can we help baby panda?

Pelican said, "I can spend days flying over the forest to see if I can find baby pandas, mother."

"Would you really do that for me?" the baby panda asked.

"Of course. Tell me everything about your home and mother. Then you should rest tonight. I will start the search tomorrow morning."

Baby panda hugged the pelican and said, "Thank you so much."

Pelican answered, "I am happy to help."

"Come," said baby harp seal. "We will sleep in my hut."

When morning arrived, pelican said, "Baby panda, stay here with all our neighbors. They will keep you safe until I return."

The pelican flew over mountains searching for the baby panda's home. Pelican searched, high and low but saw no sign of a mother panda.

Darkness came, so Pelican journeyed back.

When the pelican returned, baby panda asked, 'Did you see anything?"

The Pelican said, "No, but that doesn't mean I won't find her. I will search in another, direction tomorrow."

Eventually, we will find your mother, and you will love giving her a big, hug."

"Yes," the baby panda said, "I am grateful to have met all of you."

"Come on, baby Panda, let us go for a walk, so we can visit with all our neighbors," said baby harp seal.

"Okay," said baby Panda, "I love meeting new friends."

The harp seal guided the baby panda. They saw many more animals before they realized, it was getting late.

"What are you two doing here in the dark?" asked

the fireflies.

Baby harp seal said, "Just showing baby panda around our neighborhood."

Baby panda asked, "Where did you get those lights?"

"This is our shield for night-time flight," they answered.

"Wow," said baby panda, "I have never seen anything like this."

"We will show you everything. This is a different part of our world," the fireflies said.

"Yes, so much to learn, I am happy to have all of you as friends," replied baby panda.

On the following day, baby panda and baby harp seal took a morning walk along the shore.

Baby panda gathered all kinds of unusually colored shells.

"These are surely beautiful," he said as they continued exploring for the rest of the day.

"It's so beautiful here. The water glitters. It makes me happy."

"Yes, we live in this impressive place," the baby harp seal agreed.

Baby panda ran out to touch the water and play in the waves. "Oh my, there are other, things in here with me," baby panda shouted.

"Of course," replied the baby harp seal. "These are more of our neighbors. They live in the water and do not come on land. They are called fish; they will not hurt you."

"They are probably just as amazed as you are. They don't see many of your kind here."

Baby panda played in the water for hours. Soon, it was getting dark. So, they returned just in time to see pelican flying back. The pelican flew in from another direction.

"Anything yet?" asked baby panda.

"Sorry. Nothing today, but don't give up hope. We still have more territory to cover," pelican explained.

On the next day, baby panda awoke and noticed bugs on him.

"Oh, baby harp seal, "What are these things?" panda asked.

"They are called ladybugs. Aren't they beautiful," replied the harp seal. "They will not hurt you. They are curious. They have never seen anything like you before."

We are all learning that we can make friends everywhere, don't you agree?

"Yes," baby panda answered. "But I still wish I was with my mother."

Baby harp seal said," Pelican will not give up until he finds her. So do not worry. We are here to help you."

"Yes, I am so thankful for all the help I am getting," replied baby panda.

Fireflies were passing by and heard what was happening; they asked, "Is there anything?

We can help with?"

Pelican said, "Why yes, I could continue searching after dark if you will light the way for me."

"Then you have got it we are happy to help."

Flying together, the bird and the bugs went in a new direction, and like magic, the fireflies lit the path.

Pelican said, "Having you here sure helps me see better at night. Thanks for joining me."

"We are happy to help you and baby panda in your search for his mother," The fireflies said.

They flew for many hours without rest.

At last, the fireflies suggested, "Let's take a break."

"Sounds good to me," said the pelican.

They rested until it was daylight, and they started searching again. They searched all day until they noticed a large panda bear crying in the forest. Pelican squawked loudly to get the bear's attention.

"What is the matter?" pelican asked as he and the fireflies landed nearby.

"My son wandered off days ago. "I am worried that something may have happened to him," she replied.

"We found a baby panda a few days ago. Would you like to come with us and see if it is your son?

"Yes, I would like that very much. How long will we be?"

"It is getting late now," said the pelican. "We can guide you there and bring you back before dark if we start first thing in the morning."

The following day was beautiful and sunny as the

pelican fireflies and the mother all traveled to the ocean shore.

Baby panda saw his mother coming and rushed to meet her, yelling, "Mama, I have missed you so much."

His mother was in tears as she ran out to hug him.

"Mama, these are my friends," baby panda told his mother as all the animals he had met gathered around. "They helped me."

"I am thankful to all of you," replied Mama Panda.

Baby panda said, "I don't know what I would have done without you all. You made me feel safe during the scariest time of my life. I love you and will never forget you."

"We'd better get going so we can get you back home before dark," said the Pelican.

All baby panda's new friends ran up to hug him, then waved goodbye as they returned to their homes.

Mama panda said to baby panda, "Cherish these friends. They protected you like one of their own. This is a precious gift, my son."

They were very good to me they made me feel safe and loved," said baby panda.

Mama said, "This is the greatest life lesson: love and help each other."

THE END

About the Author

Poet and author Rebecca T. Urrutia attended Long Beach City College in California, earning her associate degree in Radio/TV Broadcasting/News and Journalism with Newspaper/Magazine Emphasis. She complements her professor, Cindy Frye, in Journalism.

In broadcasting, Robert Hersh, a 4-time Emmy winner director in radio and television and his second Emmy as an associate director for ABC's Wide World of Sports, in the 1984 Summer Olympics in LA.

The authors' interests include archaeology, geology, astronomy, photography, art, and music. She also enjoys the ocean, aquatic animals, and past cultures.

As a child, Rebecca found it difficult to stay indoors. She loved the feeling of fresh air on her face and enjoyed watching the animals in her surroundings. She was particularly interested in birds and squirrels, whose precious looks always caught her eye. In her later years, she found a fascination with spirituality, ancient cultures, and nature.

Writing about her life, she recently observed, "I realized my creativity was emerging. I wrote from the heart and started with poetry. I was analyzing life and conditions. I found my true passion in writing and started a collection of short stories in different genres. I am an explorer and hiker and have hiked extensively in Sedona, Arizona, and researched the Indigenous people who lived in the cliff dwellings. I also visited every cliff dwelling in Flagstaff, Sedona, Camp Verde, and Canyon de Chelly; it was amazing to see the structures still standing. Also, I have visited the Lowell Observatory in Flagstaff, Arizona. I had the opportunity to see Saturn from the Clark Telescope dome, an impressive sight."

She also authorizes a forthcoming romantic comedy, Wedding in Greece.

1. Why did the baby panda get lost?

2. Was it a good idea for baby panda to wander off alone?

3. What would you do if you were lost?

4. What did you learn from this story?

5. What can you teach others about this story?

6. Do you know your home address and parent's phone number?

The following pages are intentionally left blank for the children to draw and color.

Can you draw and color a baby panda bear? Do it on this page.

The following pages are intentionally left blank for the children to draw and color.

Can you draw and color a baby harp seal? Do it on this page.

The following pages are intentionally left blank for the children to draw and color.

Can you draw and color a Pelican?   Do it on this page.

The following pages are intentionally left blank for the children to draw and color.

Can you draw and color a Penguin?   Do it on this page.

The following pages are intentionally left blank for the children to draw and color.

Can you draw and color a flying fish? Do it on this page.

The following pages are intentionally left blank for the children to draw and color.

Can you draw and color shells of all colors? Do it on this page.

The following pages are intentionally left blank for the children to draw and color.

Can you draw and color Fireflies? Do it on this page.

The following pages are intentionally left blank for the children to draw and color.

Can you draw and color Ladybugs? Do it on this page.

The following pages are intentionally left blank for the children to draw and color.

Can you draw and color a fish that lives in the water? Do it on this page.

The following pages are intentionally left blank for the children to draw and color.

Can you draw and color a baby panda and mama panda bear? Do it on this page.

The following pages are intentionally left blank for the children to draw and color.

Can you draw color all of Baby Panda's friends as they wave goodbye? Do it on this page.

The following pages are intentionally left blank for the children to draw and color.

Can you draw your mother and father? Do it on this page.

The following pages are intentionally left blank for the children to draw and color.

Can you draw your home? Do it on this page.

The following pages are intentionally left blank for the children to draw and color.

Can you draw and color a rainbow? Do it on this page.

The following pages are intentionally left blank for the children to draw and color.

Can you draw hearts? Do it on this page.

The following pages are intentionally left blank for the children to draw and color.

Can you draw and color your friends? Do it on this page.

The following pages are intentionally left blank for the children to draw and color.

Can you draw and color your pet's?

The following pages are intentionally left blank for the children to draw and color.

The following pages are intentionally left blank for the children to draw and color.

The following pages are intentionally left blank for the children to draw and color.

The following pages are intentionally left blank for the children to draw and color.

The following pages are intentionally left blank for the children to draw and color.

The following pages are intentionally left blank for the children to draw and color.

The following pages are intentionally left blank for
the children to draw and color.

The following pages are intentionally left blank for the children to draw and color.

The following pages are intentionally left blank for the children to draw and color.

The following pages are intentionally left blank for the children to draw and color.

The following pages are intentionally left blank for the children to draw and color.

The following pages are intentionally left blank for the children to draw and color.

The following pages are intentionally left blank for the children to draw and color.

The following pages are intentionally left blank for the children to draw and color.

The following pages are intentionally left blank for the children to draw and color.

The following pages are intentionally left blank for the children to draw and color.

The following pages are intentionally left blank for
the children to draw and color.

The following pages are intentionally left blank for
the children to draw and color.

The following pages are intentionally left blank for
the children to draw and color.

The following pages are intentionally left blank for the children to draw and color.